This astonishing new collection from poet Bethany Lee weaves the thread of her keen attention around life's joys and sorrows, draws them tightly together and offers them into our hands. With unflinching courage she extracts beauty from her journeys as seafarer and grief-tender, makes her way into the present moment, and invites us to come along.

Her musicality and mystic's heart sing, and underneath these lines beats the steady pulse of love. *The Breath Between* offers good company for hard days, water for the thirsty spirit, and a summons to inhabit your own life more fully. You will not regret the time you spend in the chapel of these words.

More Praise for *The Breath Between*

The Breath Between is magic, pure and simple. Bethany Lee holds your hand in the suspended and infinite space between the breaths. She beckons you to pause. To be still. To reflect. With her subtle, quiet tour guide badge, she leads you along and shows you the sights and sounds and soul of your own life—the tiny things you may have forgotten, folded, as they are, between what's Significant and Large and Demanding Attention. Isn't it easy to skip over the molecules that make up the whole, as though those tiny building blocks aren't, in fact, everything? *The Breath Between* is a devotional for this modern life. It's a secret treasure map that soothes the mind and opens the heart while you remember you, too, deserve to fully breathe.

Beth Woolsey
Mess Maker, Magic Finder,
Rule Breaker, Kindness Monger

"We are mystics all," Bethany declares, with an invitation to travel with her into deep forests and inky waters, to follow stars and our own longings, wounds, and joys where, surprisingly, we discover the Light, which has been present all along. This lovely volume provides sustenance for any sojourner exploring the mysterious, wondrous workings of God in and around us.

Lisa Graham McMinn
author of *To The Table: A Spirituality
of Food, Farming, and Community*

Caught in the feel of now, negotiating time's touch, *The Breath Between* reads simple and lovely and true. Bethany Lee explores the sweet ties that bind, but also the mystery at the secret heart of each of us.

Jennifer Kemnitz
former managing editor of *Voicecatcher*

I feel I have not just now read a collection of poems. I feel instead that I have walked through a collection of moments, each of which gently called me to step into its world; invited me to meet its delicately-painted framework with my own colors, my own pain, my own dreams; and convinced me to stay for a while. The urge to race on to each next page, to see what world awaited me there, was overcome by a compulsion to allow my body just a few more breaths in the universe of the last.

Shannon Curtis
music-maker & storyteller

The Breath Between reflects Bethany Lee's significant gifts as a musician, and each poem in this collection is like the best songs, with beautiful imagery that makes us see and understand the world differently. Lee's poems challenge us to notice: to notice forests and mountains, the delight of a summer evening, the sacred spaces in our everyday lives. Each poem also turns on the axis of love, and on a recognition that choosing love over fear and condemnation is choosing life, freedom, joy. *The Breath Between* reckons with gratitude, and I am grateful to have read this collection and to be changed by the poems Lee offers to us.

Melanie Springer Mock
author of *Worthy: Finding Yourself in
a World Expecting Someone Else*

Memorization is not my strong-suit, but this collection contains so many gems I want to hold forever (including one in particular that may be my favorite poem of all time), that it begged me to commit these to memory. Packed with lines of breathtaking beauty, it left me rapturous and winded.

Benjamin Gorman
author of *Don't Read This Book* and *The Sum of Our Gods*

The first poem in Bethany Lee's collection, *The Breath Between*, welcomes us: "Let us be here together." I don't think I've ever been so delighted to accept. And when I read "How to Navigate at Night", I'm pretty sure that Bethany has been with me on the deck of my boat on night watch as we crossed one ocean or another. And isn't that the chiefest joy of poetry? To find that the writer's heart has been here together with you all along, no matter where you found yourself?

Laureen Hudson
acquisitions editor at Paper Angel Press

I don't usually understand poetry, but she's my sister, she's smart, and a great writer.

Aaron Dunlop, Ph.D.

The poems in Bethany Lee's new book, *The Breath Between*, beg to be read multiple times. With subsequent readings these mystical poems begin to burrow. Bethany writes of the search for self and the longing for belonging, of groping in the dark and of discovering "the light is always falling/falling into place." Images of sea, forest, and stars overhead, of snails and broken relationships, messages in road signs and "witness marks" all converge as testimony that "Either none of it matters/…. Or all of it/You, too."

Nancy Thomas
author of *Close to the Ground*

The Breath Between is not a book for everyone. It is a book for you. With each carefully crafted piece, Bethany beautifully weaves a message that is as simple as it is exquisite. Bethany's words will follow you home from the page and stir in your heart leaving you both curious and satisfied. Buy this book. No, buy two.

Nathalie Hardy

I can't help but remember my own wonder, my own joy, when Bethany shares these vivid word pictures of gratitude, curiosity, and witness. Already, I'm adding her poems to the ones I read to keep faith and stay open-hearted. And I will share this beautiful book with kindred friends who will deeply enjoy it too!

Melanie Weidner

artist and spiritual director

Bethany Lee's *The Breath Between* invites readers into a spaciousness in day-to-day living that can help us see the wonder that shimmers in ordinary moments. Her lovely images and experiences draw us to notice, to be present, to create breathing room.

Howard R. Macy

author of *Rhythms of the Inner Life:*
Yearning for Closeness with God

The Breath Between

An Invitation to Mystery and Joy

Bethany Lee

For Jillian
Breathe
Bethany Lee

Fernwood
PRESS

The Breath Between

An Invitation to Mystery and Joy

©2019 by Bethany Lee

Fernwood Press
Newberg, Oregon
www.fernwoodpress.com

Printed in the United States of America

Cover and interior design: Mareesa Fawver Moss

Cover photo: Eric Muhr

Author photo: Bee Joy España

ISBN 978-1-59498-061-9

For Mom and Dad, who loved me into being
And for Bryan, who loves me into becoming

Contents

Prelude

Poetry
brings
present
that
which
is
apart

Let
us
be
here
together

Door to Door

I assume you live
In a home with a sign
A placard by your entry
"No Solicitors"

Yet here I stand
Knocking anyway
Ready to offer
Care and quiet listening
Bread and poetry
And the exquisite noticing

How can I know if you are napping
Or otherwise not prepared
To receive visitors?

Maybe you are engaged
In your own work
Of painting or repairing or love making
And you do not need what I have to offer

Maybe you are grieving
And cannot stand up from the floor
To come to the entryway

Try to be polite if you
Must shut the door between us

But if you want to make an exchange—
For I need your gifts in return
If you need what it is I hold
Let me in
Oh, let me in

As Long as a Life

Sometimes I go
To the abbey near my house
In search of sacred space
And silence
In the air are dust motes
Dragonflies and sung prayer

At the edge of the pond
At the foot of the hill
There is a quiet room
A wall of windows at one end
Cushions and kneeling benches
In a neat grid on the floor

From my seat I can see
A row of tidy white crosses
Near the monk's quarters
And a stand of old trees
Evergreen, collected
Each moment
I choose where to turn my gaze

As long as a life
Within sight of one's end
Colors the present vividly
Fosters hope and not despair
Keep your eyes on the grave

But if the nearness of death
Stokes fear
And spins a frantic striving
Look away for a time
Sit as pupil beneath the cedars
Learn the long grace
Of those who rise
Live so freely in one place
And then fall

Who even after death
Release their essence
Nourish so well
With their letting go

At Summer's End

We who sleep through the nights
May forget to count them

And rain fell on the earth
Forty days and forty nights

But the watchers, the vigil-keepers
Those who toil in the shadows
And the new-made mothers
Never forget
That half a day is darkness

And there was evening
And there was morning
The first day

Half a tree is underground
Half a breath is exhalation

Receive
Release
Receive
Release

The Son of Man will be
Three days and three nights
In the heart of the earth

Be not dismayed at the waning light

See the women, sitting
Under a moon so bright
Even the shadows are illumined

There's darkness, yes
But it's that of roots
Of loam, of the deep
Where all things grow

They are weaving in the moonlight
Not tomorrow's shift
Or next year's covering
Day brings space enough for the practical

No, tonight they weave the extravagant
Wind the dearest salvaged pieces
Into gossamer too fine to handle

If it's not for covering the table
Or wicking up the spilled
Why take the time?

You know, don't you, why the weavers toil till dawn
On a work that will not last the night?

Some things are too precious to be held

First Person, Plural

In the years before I became singular
And the days rolled out for us
Like a bolt of pressed cotton
Our grandmother stitched the pattern
Diamonds and flowers, honeycombs

Out in the garden
We bit raspberries from our fingertips
And eyed the foxglove warily
While our grandfather climbed the apple tree
We ate well and drank from the white cup
The last thick drops of old coffee

We grew tired
We were escorted through the cloud
Of camphor by the bathroom sink
Teeth cleaned
Taken into the back room
Where the cold always gathered
Rolled onto linen sheets
And piled over with quilts

We were kissed
We were interred with ceremony
A hand to our heads
The turning of the switch
The silent settling of the door
Into its place at the jamb

But the sweetness remained at the threshold
As if it meant to spend the night standing near

A snail winds
Her own home
From what she encounters
On the way

Coils from the earth
A shell of stone
Safety for her softness
Ever larger at the edges

If she traveled faster
She might miss
The gifts that came her way
It takes time to transform
Dust into shelter

The channel is clogged
Silt drifted
Down
On spring floodwaters
And settled
Where the deepwater ships must go

Slowly
And all the work is underwater
Sand enough
To build a new land
Sucked, spat
Onto flat barge behind

This earth served upriver
Displaced it impedes

See how the water wants to flow?
Surface sparkling
Pulsing near the edges
Still center deep

When I come, mistaken
Thinking that you want to take
The place where I am standing
Wondering if your song
Will silence mine
Afraid I need to shout you down
To speak my own truth
I quail and we are both thrust
Into the sudden darkness

In laughter, I remember
My essence is my own
And also it is one with yours
Which is your own in turn

It is a grand absurdity
For the waves to wrestle over
Who can be the sea
For the winds to war about
Which makes up the air

I choose
to live, move, and have my being
held in the orbit around
the presence at the center of love

Forgetting the need for careful balance
I sling out into the turning
all else blurring at the edge of my sight
face full to the blowing wind

No longer afraid of letting
someone go free
without enough condemnation
No longer afraid
to be free indeed

I need not strive
to live out a different metaphor
or fear love is too small a story

I choose
to narrow my narrative
to the infinite

When they burn the papers
And pull the plug
On half the truth
Always the worst half
And sit, bereft and blinking
In the sudden silence
And fear

I want to be the one who speaks
And rhymes love with love

When the weary marchers take to the streets
With no voices anymore
Hoarse from shouting at the wall
And done with the violence of rage
And the rage of violence
And they drop their fists and wonder
And wander toward the edges

I want to be the one who sings
And rhymes love with love with love

When the unimaginative have imagined the unimaginable again
And the camps come for us
And the fences wind themselves around our bodies
And none of it worked
And everything failed
And hope was a mirage in a desert of tears
And all is lost but loss and the ashes
Of the lives that blazed in beauty and in joy
And some are beginning to remember to decide to hold hands anyway
(And some never stopped remembering to hold hands anyway)
And some are bearing witness while others give away their bread

We will be the ones, with poetry in our hearts
Who rhyme love with love with love with love with love with love with love

Andante

I walked into the woods
Laid down beneath the trees
And rested my hands on the moss
I let the sun settle
And waited
Until the wild rabbits
Came out of the hedge
Until my ears cleared
And the silence of the forest
Spread across the ground
I waited
There on the edge of something new
Until the birds began to sing again
Until I began to believe
There was time enough
For all of it
And I breathed in the sweetness
Of crushed mint and wild blackberries

What I Hope Comes After

On a summer evening when all had gathered
And poured their love in the same direction
And together they wove a beauty of listening
While the players played
So joyfully that everyone danced

At the end of the evening
As the sun began to set
The last encore stretched out
And laid her hand on each one's head

Everything stepped into
The hush of surrender
Where the silence breathes for you
And in that moment
There was no need for applause
Only yes and this amen

The Breath Between

Is not the space between the breaths

(Breathe the breath between)

When the old monk was almost done with his body

Already done with his watch
You run out of time before the end, it seems
Before you run out the time

Done with feet
Done with hands
He will not again walk from this place
Or make

To be caught in now
So completely
Looks like loss

Does it feel like loss to him?
Does it feel like a gift?
Like the shape of being held?

This is the breath between the question and the answer

The breath between the bread and the wine
After the thanks has been given
Before the nourishment received

(Breathe the breath between)

Where else do you find this breath hiding?
How do you pick it up?
Breathe it in and let it go?

Can you name it?
Can you name this breath?

Call it here
Call it holy
Call it home

Please forgive the space left empty

The poem that was meant for this page

Is not my verse to share
Though I set the story to words
The tune belongs to another

Here, I would have played of beauty
And of the loss of beauty
Of love and grief laid side by side

And yet, already, you are turning
To the place in your heart
Where the knowledge of this song is stored

Please forgive the space left empty
Perhaps you may find here on this leaf
Notes on your own silent elegy

Moon Round

When all is shaken
Turn your face to the moon
Though you may need to kneel
And bow your head
To the other side of the earth

Waxing crescent
first quarter
waxing gibbous
full

Waning gibbous
third quarter
waning crescent
new

Sing her a song of her reborn self
How she hangs in the sky all over the world
Sometimes on end like an outstretched hand
some places scooped like a begging bowl

Waxing crescent
first quarter
waxing gibbous
full

Waning gibbous
third quarter
waning crescent
new

The pull of the moon slows our spinning
Yet this is only as it should
How could it be that this great turning
Would not bring us closer to stillness?

Waxing crescent
first quarter
waxing gibbous
full

Waning gibbous
third quarter
waning crescent
new

How to Navigate at Night

To Touch the Face of God

Pick a likely looking star
Wonder for a moment if you've chosen a planet

Be still

Hold the wind on one side of your face

Be

more still

Check your compass course carefully

Let go of what is keeping you
from being fully present

Settle your vessel into a steady rhythm
Wave and swell, gust and lull

Breathe

Look calmly into the darkness for what there is to see

Look calmly into the darkness
For what there is to see

Find a point of reference amidst all that is moving:
the silver shrouds glinting in the moonlight
the dark spot at the top of the oscillating mast

Remember you are a brilliant point of radiance
Everything that is
is made of light

Angle your vision until the celestial body
approaches your reference point

Don't lose sight of what you're doing here

Steer gently, fearlessly
The whole ship turns on a tiny lever

Return to your breath; return to being

Let the ancient light of the faraway star
Come near enough to lead you home

Burn with the ageless flame of the eternal sun
Become the light that leads you home

It's a curious thing, but it feels like the present

Yes
This matters
This cup of tea
This body
This morning
This stuffy nose
These words

Either none of it matters
    The earthquakes and the weddings
    The light bill and the babies
    The ocean and the stars
    And the endings and
    The bleeding hearts

Or all of it
You, too

Caesura

Driving home last evening
A hot July day
With the green vines still
Abiding on the hills
And the moon rising almost
Full at my back
Two birds flew, dipping
One swooped too low
And caught my speed
And fell

The poor will always be with us
The sparrows will never stop falling
But larger hands are beneath us
Returning the fallen to flight

Along with all the Broken Pieces

"You will be reconciled," I heard
"It's only a matter of when."

So I wrote the letter that got no reply
Smiled across the way at the store
Didn't duck down the next aisle

And as I did
I held for us both the certainty of wholeness

Because I can see it so clearly
So clearly
The way we will one day
In this world or a new one
Laugh and cry together
At the silly ways our hurt
And keen grief kept us apart

We will rejoice at the reuniting

What a powerful capacity
Seeing what is not yet
but *will be*

I can feel it taking shape
No, it has already taken shape
It is the truest becoming

Allegro

These branches
in your way are just
doing their job
They don't grow here
to block your path
It's the nature of fear to stop you
Hold you still
Keep you from the deeper way
Don't fight
Clear your way with love
Gentle steps and slow
Wonders await further in

Signs of Life

Free to a good home

Take one

Attention!

Have you seen this person?

Children at play

Caution, people at work, slow down

Be on the lookout

Lost and Found

Please watch where you step

Notice

To Myself

I belong from a family of Scotland
From Ireland and England
Island people and seafarers

I belong from the ones who went west
From Oklahoma and Michigan
From the ones who came on the Oregon Trail
From the girl in a tent in the logging camp
Next to the grand Columbia

I belong from the ones who met
Making music together and never stopped
Who wrote my name at the very first
And carried me as long as I needed

I belong from the one who taught me to climb trees
Who built forts and wrote codes and drove me across town
And drove away when the time came

I belong for the one, chosen of heart
Who carried me west beyond the shores of my home
For the one who showed me the Southern Cross
And remains with me in a life of our own making

I belong for my daughters who are becoming from me

I belong with the dearest always friends
Who walk so near
I belong here in this web of belonging
We hold these threads for each other
Each of us at our own center

A Quintessence

I say that we are wound
with mercy round and round
as if with air

—Gerard Manley Hopkins,
"The Blessed Virgin"

We the mystics were not surprised
by the discovery of dark matter
We could have told you all along
what we can see is not all there is

When will there be a scope sensitive enough
for mercy's sake?
What instrument could be deployed to measure it
and what would the units be?
A sweetness of mercy?

If we could measure mercy in mothers
like we count engine strength in horse power
gather it in buckets,
transfer it in pipelines,
would we deplete its source?
Strip it from the air
and leave the poor bereft?
Or could we deem it a self-sustaining resource?

The giving of mercy yields mercy
We breathe it in and out
as the trees breathe air
We are made ever richer
I believe
in the exchange

If this is Jubilee
What land will I restore?
What debts erase?
And to what ancestral home
Shall I return?

If Jubilee is yet to come
May my hands stay open
And my heart stay free
May I live without indenturing
Myself to you
Or you to me

Was forty years not enough time
To learn to trust provision?
Manna, every day
And twice on Fridays

To light a candle without a prayer
Takes a practiced inattention

It's hard work to listen to children laughing
Revel in a perfect melon
Watch the dusk fade into night
Without feeling the soul respond

This requires
Clenching my heart shut
Holding my spirit's breath
Pursing the lips of my soul

When will I relax into fearlessness
Breathe again the natural inhalation of mystery
And be at peace?

Partial Eclipse

Last night in my sleep
I dreamed of gentle hands
Smoothing back hair
Soothing
A mother's touch

I came to know
With the clarity of a dreamer
These hands were my own hands
And they were safe
And necessary

They moved with purpose
Finding wounds and noticing
The places healing had already begun

They came suddenly away
From familiar terrain
To the thick line
Of an old scar

How had I not noticed this before?
How could I have borne this pain
And the mending that came after
Beyond the reach of memory?

Awake, I go looking
Match my fingertips to their unwoken selves
The scar is gone, its toughness
Only remains in quickly fading recollection

West of west
Wind at my back
Belly of fear
At the climbing swell
Night fall, mist rise
No moon, no stars in the sky

A hymn dislodged
From the bones of my feet
Where childhood days
Had wedged it
Rose through trembling legs
Flew through lungs
And poured out my open mouth

Sound fell to silence
Each note dropped
Dropped
Onto another wave
Ran alongside
And sank in my wake

Because no one was listening
The fear flowed out with the love
The dark received the song of itself

But there in the deep
It rose back to me, carried
In the mouths of the great sea dancers
Illuminated by presence

They stripped the hymn of its fear
Left only the blessings behind
Flung them back in the boat at my feet
And followed
Tossed them, whistling, over the boom
Followed through the night
Flicking the stars from their tails

Drawn from the Safe

It was the first time she was brave enough
to say what she wanted
How had it taken so long?

Girls weren't supposed to need
Girls weren't supposed to ask

No one had ever accused her of being high-maintenance
But what was so bad about a little more maintenance?
What was so bad about admitting
how much time and energy
the simple tasks of a whole life could require?

So she asked for what she needed and paid for it
paid the price
paid attention
What are you saving for?
Life costs everything

Notice joy
The way your heart
lifts in your chest
with hope at the robin's return
Perhaps this
is what the wishbone is for

Allow space for the pang
The hand around the heart
at the sight of a purpled leaf
A beauty too extravagant

This is how you can know
you are one of humanity
Build your tolerance
for what astounds you

Be amazed
even if kneeling on holy ground
means risking the thorns
in your bared soul
Do not fear the pain of being
wide awake to glory

Hear now, the chickadee call
Watch the fog
lift from the lake
There it is
in your own breath
sustenance and mystery

Largo

Signal Flare

Though I walk to the mountain alone
and there rest in a shelter of stones
hear the wind and feel the earthquake
and listen in the silence
The fire burns and lights my way
and I am not consumed

How long am I cast away to the mountain?
Away from the dance
and the market day?
Must the beacons be set aflame
so far apart?

Witness Mark, noun

Generally an intentional, accidental, or
Naturally occurring spot
Line, groove, or other
Contrasting area
That serves as
An indicator of certain facts

A high water line is a witness mark
The flood rose here and no further
The tide rolled the flotsam high
And ebbed away

In geography and surveying
A blaze, cut, hole, or message
Written on a tree, rock, or other guide
To indicate a boundary, feature, or significant point
Especially on a witness post

There on the bookshelf
A series of sentinels stand
Written word as witness post
Each a guide to indicate
A boundary, feature, or significant point

In construction and manufacturing
A line, groove, score, notch, cut, or written indicator
Made on the surface of material
To impart information
Such as where to cut or join

Wedding day as witness mark
Wedding day and birth day
And death day and burial
Witness marks litter my calendar
Stitch seams into my years
Offer a pattern
For where to cleave
To cut or join

In forensic investigation
A surface groove, smear, stain
Abrasion, or other feature
That can serve as evidence

Clockmakers use witness marks
To guide a repair
A re-pairing
The antique clock exposed on the workbench
No schematics to work from
Only the scars of use
Wear marks and grooves indicate
Original intent
Fit and design

And my scars?
Do they speak to the way
I am to be put back together?

From What Remains

Behind all connection
Is the challenge of loving work,
Opening my soul,
And silence

Rest, listen
Seek safe community
Real people
A sacramental presence
Where metaphor reflects mystery

Gathered friends by the sea
Making music happen
Consolation for this stretch season

In wholeness flows both joy and light
A capacity for courage
Hovering in our difference

Some days
I forget how
To be a poet

At times when I
Have done too much
And rested too little

When I am worried
And my fretful mind
Is consumed
With everything that might be
And nothing that is

My pen scribbles
And runs dry
And I can't find the well within

On those days
I can still feel the empty place
Inside
A room with no doors
Where there is calm
Quiet
At the center
Nothing to knock on
No one to let you in

Some days I remember how to walk through walls

Altar

The gods of the woods demand their sacrifice
    I pour it out—black, shiny, anointed
    and stand back

They are fickle, these gods, capricious
    unaffected by my yearning nearness

They come at their own whim
    leave on their own command
They deign to accept my offering
    too high above my station to meet my eye

"Back!" say their beaks on the glass between us
    "Back!" beat their wings on the window frame
    "You are not worthy to approach the altar."

They spread their royal robes wide
    snap them regally into place
    Black crowns never slip from glossy heads

Morning prayers and evening prayers
    Twice a day I stop to bow

Common Wealth

Every year
He brings home new color
Whatever catches his eye at the garden store
Arranges it around
The evergreen bushes in the bed
Keeps them watered when I forget

Once, one of last year's batch
Proved perennial
And sprouted proud
Just beyond this year's yield
An awkward joke of a corner

He tends the rosemary especially
Eight steps across the yard
To dip his fingers
Into the clinging scent
Shares the harvest willingly
For my more interior pursuits

We follow the same rule:
Always embrace what you really love
Which takes your breath away
With its softness or its fall

Inside and out
What we love takes shape
And gives shape
A common wealth for all who yearn

This year, hummingbirds

At the Rise in the Road

(where I always remember to breathe)

Oh, green western woods
and eastern filbert tree geometry

Your light never fails at perfecting

Filtered through the fog in fall
Gently golden on late summer evenings

A crisp, spring spotlight shines
on this year's crimson clover crop

Hush, we will not speak of winter
for winter is the season of silence

From behind the willowed brook
comes the scent of surrender

Once, you sheltered doe and fawn
beneath your holy dome

Once, and never since
though you call this grace to mind each time
and breath lifts away to follow

Though silence
Can be a form
Of worship
Let us not
Resort to it
From the fear
Of getting God
Wrong

We must keep essaying
Keep finding God hidden
In all the wrong places
And a few of the right ones

When I see God in everything
In an orange peel
And the stained glass
In the fried chicken and biscuits
And the bread and wine
And when you see God in nothing
Never fully incarnate
In this shattered universe
We are both of us
Kneeling at the same altar

Composing a Life

The photographer composes
By the rule of thirds
The painter composes a still life
With the fruit of the harvest
An empty bowl
Whatever is to hand

The practice always more
About the seeing than the sight

Wordsmiths, too, craft a composition
Hammering away with pen and ink
Tossing a few more sticks on the fire
Adding space for breath and flame
Working the medium in the red-hot moment
Then polishing, polishing the tarnish away

A musician composes hope
Makes a work for another day
That comes to life only
When gut and wood and hair and wind
Begin to cast their earthly magic

The work of one's hands is a holy thing
The art of a life seen in thirds
Near enough to others for harmony
Bears a fruit worth contemplation
Offers daily grace to the composer

And also to—
What is the word for the one who receives the art?
The one to whom the composition is offered?

What do you call
The one who stands
Or sits
Or kneels
Or bows with open hands?
The one who is both composer
And recipient of this work called life?

What is the word that can tell the whole?
Is it grateful?

Enough Already

(For the women of 2018)

Turn on the lights
Make some tea
Feed the birds
While the kettle boils
Light a candle
Wear soft clothes
And a soft sweater
Call a friend
Pick a couple of weeds
Just that one, there
Maybe that one, too
Gently
Don't make yourself finish
A hard job today
Play a little
Eat something delicious
And perhaps something nourishing
Gently, gently
As if you believed you were a darling
Worthy
Beautiful soul
Full of being enough

Liturgy

Just once so far this season
Has the great egret been there
At the bend in the road
By the edge of the water

But the watching for her
The every day catch in my throat
At the possibility of this time—

The watching is wonder enough

Finale

It was a night like this, at the end of summer. The waning moon had not yet risen so we found our way out by the light of the stars, surprisingly bright in the lush evening. The warm night breeze did all the things night breezes are best at, caressed skin, stroked faces, lifted hair and spirits.

There is no magic incantation to call forth a night like this. No matter what charm you have spoken, what hexes woven, there will be a day you must wake up with sorrow. And all that work of staying present in the moment will feel like wasted practice in an hour of keening pain.

How many perfect moments will one life allow? How will I know when I have run out? Or do they bloom like raspberries, ripening all summer long as I take the time to pluck and savor, shriveling up and going dormant when no one pays attention anymore.

We stopped at the tideline to slip off our shoes and tuck up our pants, the one-legged stork dance ridiculous in the dark. We dragged the rowboat down to the water and waited for the swell to rise, in a single uplifting wave. A rush of limbs and oars and we bore away, stroking for the light from the boat in the bay. Everywhere the oars touched, sparks rang out, green drops like fireflies scattered. I dipped my hand behind the stern and watched the wake of tiny stars. The echo of sea creatures sloped away to the depths.

It was a night like this, at the end of summer and there would never be another. So as soon as we reached the shelter of the boat, we stripped and set out again, leaping this time into the ink—great angels of light in the deep.

Answering the Question

But how can I begin
to tell about that primal day in Soyatán
where the springs of the ancient
earth mingled with the freshness
of that summer's fertility
and no one really knew
anymore what the stone carvings meant
but over in the wooden church
they stitched the sword to the angel's side
so it wouldn't fall again
and wreak another miracle?

Or what about the day
the rain poured down
after so many months without
and we stood by the river's edge
and you welcomed us home
and the rain poured down?

What can I say about the night
in the pool when the silky water ran
soft across my thighs
my belly, my breasts, my throat
and promises already being kept
were spoken aloud and heard?

How can I tell you
what it meant to feel
a slick new body slip from mine
and fall back
triumphant, bereft?

But I must keep trying
to say these things because
you inhabit them too
you have your own
moments of wonder
so powerful you can almost not
bear to look at them

We are mystics all
Let us look together
I'll go first and you can look with me
then I will gaze with you into
the bright sun of your own knowing

Close to the Dawn

A delicate refining
Melted the used to be
Into a strong new cadence
The way the light is always falling
Falling into place

Hope left a shimmer
In her wake
I didn't know we were
So close to the dawn
Where the light is always falling
Falling into place

At the heart of dark uncertainty
Lies a delicious curiosity
From that grows
A capacity to openness
A capacity for love

Light has come
And the darkness is befriended
That day, a hymn of joy
Flew across the eastern sky
For the light is always falling
Falling into place

From the Inside

From across the way
It isn't clear
If she's laughing
Or crying

Her face contorts
Or crinkles
And her mouth falls open
I hear her gasping for breath
And wonder
Does she want to be comforted
Or alone in her joy?

I have heard the unmistakable sounds
Of deepest grief
I will not tell of it here
You know it already—or not
In the center of your being

Can you rend the sky with laughter as well as with pain?

I look away
She needs no witness to this vivid moment
Life is lived from the inside
Hearts shy as the wild

In the Wilderness

The leaders we find it easy to follow
Who stride ahead with certainty and power
Are taking us to a land
Where we think we want to go

But those who walk with stumbling steps
Slow and careful in the darkness
These accompany us into the promised land
To the place we already are
Into the place that is already home

Moving

Ants count steps to find their way home

Honeybees dance to point the way to sweetness

Dung beetles orient by the Milky Way

Trees grow more on the shadow side
Bending always to the light

A Nautilus steals salt from the sea
Jets backward on the ocean floor

Maple seeds spin their way down to fertile ground

Glaciers flow

Squirrels leap

Spiders swing from spun silk

Migratory birds see with different eyes
Read the earth's magnetic field like a map

Cottonwoods blow on the wind, fall to earth far away

Dragonflies swim up from the mud
Split their skin and the roof of their world
Grow wings in time to find the sky

Age turns healing on its head

First, the wounds of a moment
Those which would have healed
Overnight on our childhood fingers
The paper cut, the hangnail
These begin to linger

Next, new pains sprout up from nowhere
With no impact, bruises blossom
We awake to new insults
Stiff feet and sore hips
The cough extends its unwelcome stay

I hear that at some point
Things begin to fall apart completely
A disintegration
If we have not practiced trusting
What truly holds us together
This will likely be disconcerting and frightful
(It will almost certainly be that anyway)
As the coming together reverses
And begins accelerating
Toward evanescence

I fall apart
It is the way of all things
Which give their lives
To nurture another

It too is the way of all things
Which cling, unsuccessfully
To themselves

If healing is a turn toward wholeness
(And I know I am just a part of the whole)
Who am I to think I can get there in one piece?
How could I ever believe I must arrive there alone?

If it's all the same with you
I'm just going to go ahead and be
joyful

To be perfectly honest
I've decided to be joyful any
way

For a long time

I've been afraid that my joy
would be misunderstood
as indifference
or selfishness

Or worse
that I would truly
be
indifferent
or selfish

It seemed joy should wait until
there wasn't a terrorist attack on the news
Until no one had AIDS or cancer or malaria
Until all the lost children had found a way home

But joy is not the antithesis of pain
Joy is not the absence of grief
Joy doesn't ignore injustice
Joy abides

Joy is the flicker
illuminating the night
and joy is the live wire
powering the light

Joy is the spark flung from the flame
drawing others to the warmth
And joy is the fuel
at the center of the fire

Count This as the Last

I am not a goddess
a psychic
or an oracle

And so it will therefore happen
that I will not notice
the day I begin
my last revolution
around the sun

Even if I could identify the moment
I kick off my final months in this incarnation
I could not then orchestrate
a perfect year

And so it will therefore happen
that I will live my last days in imperfection
and when death announces himself
months
or weeks
or moments
before his grand entrance
I may only have time
for a few quick regrets

But that would be a waste
(Please remember to remember this)
When I have had this
one
perfect
autumn
with you

To Keep Faith

Trust your bones
Trust the pull of the earth
And the earth itself
Trust the hearts of trees
The stone at the edge of the sea
And all else true

Trust that water will bear you up
Trust the moon to keep faith
With ebb and flow
Trust the leafing
The chrysalis, the seed
And every other way
Death gives birth to resurrection

Acknowledgments

For all the circles which have held me
The circle of family, ever widening
Circle of woods and earth and sea and sky

For the brilliant circles of women around me
Irene, Jenny, Maria, Tamarah—sisters by happenstance and choice
Polly, Peggy, Lisa, Jennifer, who kept me prop-rich and writing
For the McMinnville Women's Choir, who circle round to tend the fire
For all the Quaker women who listened with me
And the scattered ones whose weft holds me still—
Sue, Ashlee, Allison, Erin, Jenn

For PDXWriters, who pointed the way
For Fernwood Press, who said yes
For my favorite cheerleaders—Abram, Meika, Kesia,
Caleb, Annika, Josiah
And for Kyla and Gavin, who are saving shelf space for me

For my fellow travelers—Hannah and Meira
I am blessed to call you my daughters
For Jenn, who knows
For Mauri, unexpected gift
For Kate, always
And for Bryan, at the heart of the center with me

I am grateful

CPSIA information can be obtained
at www.ICGtesting.com
Printed in the USA
FSHW011929040519